CAMPBELL MORRIS

Best Jumbo Paper Aircraft

Illustrations:
STEPHEN CASE

Model diagrams:
CAMPBELL MORRIS &
ADENA GOLDBERG

A Perigee Book

Introduction

Welcome to the larger-than-life world of paper aircraft. My new models are not only bigger, they go further too! The term 'jumbo' is used loosely. Anything larger than 8½"x11" is certainly big, and some models use several sheets to make even bigger models. Imagine turning heads with the larger species in this book!

Making origami models, in particular paper aircraft, has always captured the interest of old and young alike. Some people in the United States are fanatical about paper aircraft, and other countries, like Spain, hold annual paper aircraft competitions for distance, performance and design.

So come with me on a new journey of paper discovery. As with my previous books, I hope the models will inspire you to create your own designs.

Happy folding and flying!

Types of Paper to Use

Most of the models in this book use 11"x17", which is twice the size of standard letter-size paper. Some models use two or more sheets attached to one another to make even larger planes. Tape and cardboard are sometimes used to enhance the rigidity of those models with wider wingspans. A suitable sheet of 11"x17" should be photocopy-strength or better.

Many of the materials needed for the models can be found around the house. One model employs empty toilet rolls while another uses the cardboard from a breakfast cereal box — items that would otherwise have been thrown out.

Protection of our environment is very important. When finished with your model, don't throw it out. Paint it with your insignia and keep it or give it to a friend. You could even make a mobile for your bedroom!

Explanation of Symbols

The following symbols are very important for successful folding. I have reduced the number of different symbols to avoid confusion. Always practise the folds with smaller sheets of paper first.

fold in direction
of arrow

turn model over

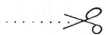

cut along dotted line

push in

repeat this procedure on
the other side
of the model

larger view

open out

fold several times

FOLD
FOLD

2

Folding Techniques

The technique of folding goes hand-in-hand with the following symbols. Grab a small piece of paper and try these tricks:

1
Valley fold Fold in direction of arrow along the line of dashes.

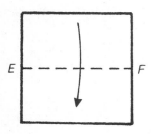

When this valley fold has a dotted line it means that the rest of the fold is hidden behind a flap.

2
Mountain fold Fold the top end behind, in direction of arrow, along the line of dots and dashes.

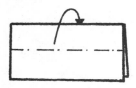

3
It should look like this (unless someone screwed it up while you weren't looking).

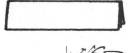

Now grab a longer piece of paper and fold it in half.

1
Inverse fold See the line of dots and dashes? Fold along this line backwards and forwards until the paper is well creased, then, holding the lower end A with thumb and finger, push in the other end B to meet the edge A.

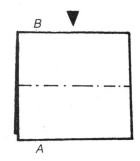

2
Yes ... it's almost there.

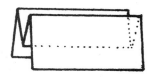

(dots show hidden fold)

3
Now flatten the paper. You have just completed an **inverse fold**. (Try doing that to someone's school books — maybe the kid who screwed up your piece of paper?)

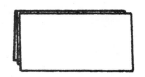

*Now we'll try a classic fold used often in making paper planes: the **water bomb base**.*

1
Water bomb base fold Fold and crease the valley folds AD and BC, then the mountain fold EF.

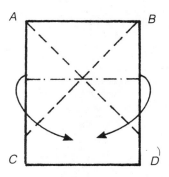

2
Place your finger in the centre where all creases meet. The paper sides should pop up. Move the sides inwards bringing the top end downwards.

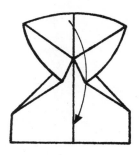

3
The completed fold.

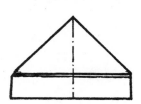

Troubleshooting

Won't fly? One way to solve the problem is to stuff all your failures into someone else's school bag and let them work it out. The better solution is to go back through all the folding steps, unfolding your glider until you strike the problem. In many cases, it's simply a lack of symmetry. Whatever you fold on the left-hand side of a piece of paper, you must do exactly the same for the right-hand side. Use a steel rule and measure distances on both sides. In time, you'll be able to judge symmetry pretty well.

Other reasons why your plane won't fly are:

- *Not thrown properly.*
- *Too windy, or thrown in wrong direction to wind.*
- *Wrong type of paper used (newspaper is definitely out).*
- *Wrong dimensions of paper used.*
- *Your model needs more tail lift. Try curling up the rear section a little.*
- *Some horribly nasty person has sabotaged your model.*

Arrow

Sherwood Forest in the classroom? It's not quite as ferocious as the wooden or aluminium versions, but this model will certainly get your message across. You will need three sheets of paper— 1 piece 11"x17", 1 piece 8½"x11" and 1 piece 5½"x8½" (half the size of 8½"x11"). Folding is simple.

1
Shaft section With an 11"x17" sheet already crease folded in half lengthwise, fold the sides in as shown to meet centre crease.

2
Fold sides in again to meet centre crease.

3
Fold sides in again, then fold in half.

4
The finished shaft.

Shaft section (11"x17")

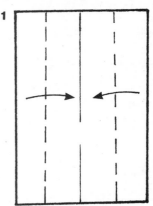

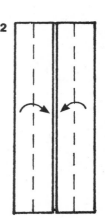

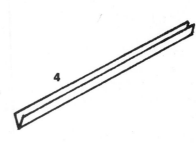

Tail wing section (8½"x11")

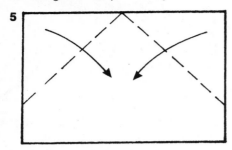

5

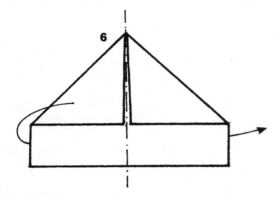

6

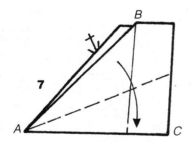

7

5

Tail wing section Using a sheet of 8½"x11" paper facing you horizontally, fold the top corners in as shown.

6

Fold in half behind.

7

Fold leading edge AB down to meet bottom edge AC. Repeat on the other side.

8

Measure ½" from base at nose end and 1½" at tail end, then fold wings down.

9

Fold wing fins, noting measurements. Lift wings up.

10

Your tail 'feathers'.

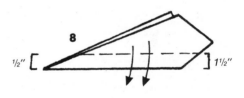

8

½"   1½"

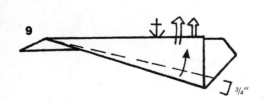

9

¾"

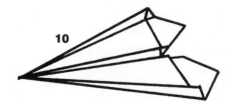

10

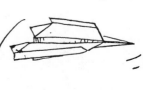

Arrowhead section (5½″x8½″)

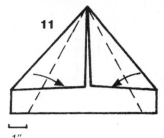

11
Arrowhead section Use a sheet of 5½″x8½″ paper (half the size of 8½″x11″) with the top corners folded in the same way as the tail wing section in step 5. Measure 1″ in from the bottom left and bottom right corners. Fold as shown.

1″

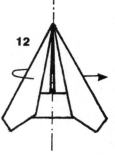

12
Fold in half behind.

13
Fold wings down in approximate position shown.

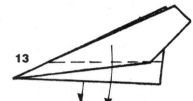

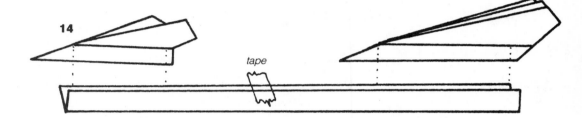

tape

14
Now let's put it all together! Arrowhead and tail slot inside the paper shaft as shown. Use small pieces of tape to secure the sections, then experiment with the model to get the best balance. When you have achieved this, use more tape to tightly secure your model.

15
Your completed Arrow.

Throwing Instructions
Throw with major force to your intended target. More thrust can be achieved by substituting a wooden or plastic rule for the paper shaft.

Stable Glider

If you prefer comfort to speed, if you're sick of those yawing, jarring junks that fill the skies, then try one of these.

1

Begin with an 11"x17" sheet spread lengthwise. Fold top right corner down to meet bottom left corner.

2

Unfold and repeat for top left corner.

3

Fold behind as shown, the crease meeting the centre of the diagonal creases. Then bring the sides in, top edge down as for the water bomb base.

4

Almost there.

5

Fold flap up in approximate position shown.

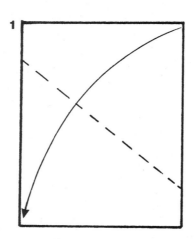

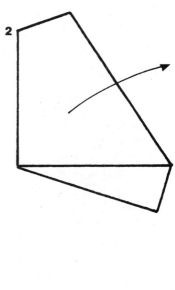

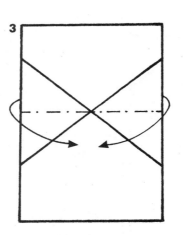

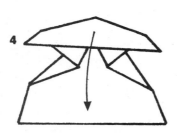

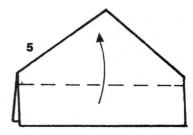

7

6
Fold flap up in half, noting left corner circled. This step is described in more detail in step 7.

7
As step 6 is performed the flap X lifts up with it.

8
Crease flat and it should look like this. Turn the model over.

9
Fold sides behind, tucking them into the hidden flaps.

10
Fold leading edge down as shown.

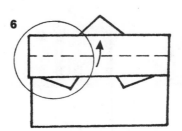

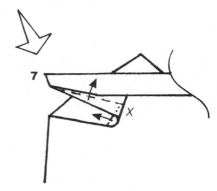

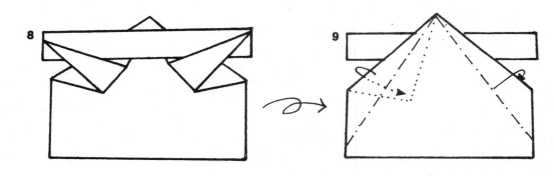

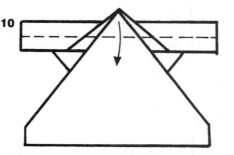

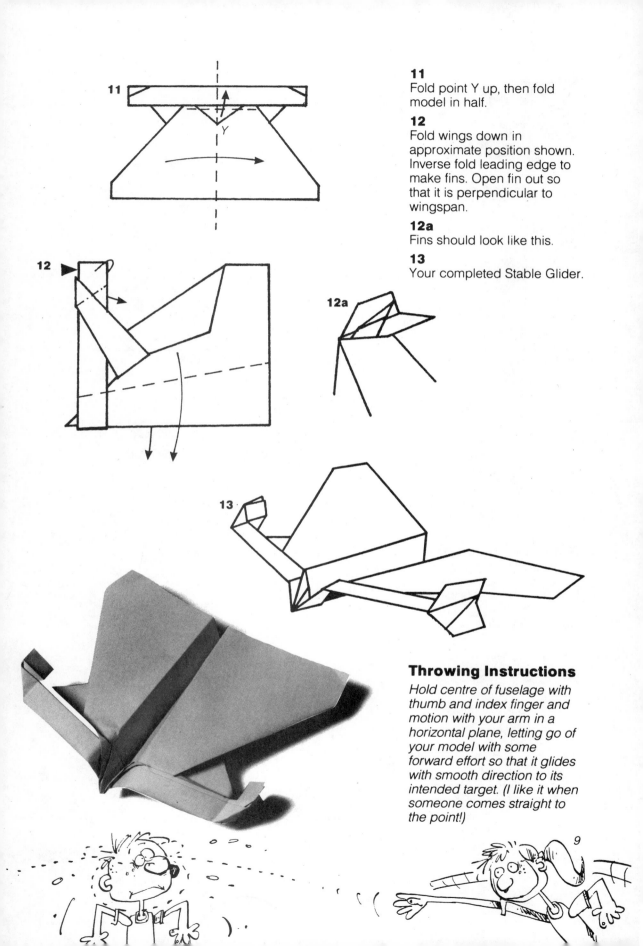

11
Fold point Y up, then fold model in half.

12
Fold wings down in approximate position shown. Inverse fold leading edge to make fins. Open fin out so that it is perpendicular to wingspan.

12a
Fins should look like this.

13
Your completed Stable Glider.

Throwing Instructions

Hold centre of fuselage with thumb and index finger and motion with your arm in a horizontal plane, letting go of your model with some forward effort so that it glides with smooth direction to its intended target. (I like it when someone comes straight to the point!)

Big Wing

Like a graceful swallow, this model will turn elegantly in a soft breeze, coming in to land who knows where? Or coming in to poop on who knows whom???

1

Begin with two sheets of 11"x17" paper. Leaving one sheet aside for the moment, fold up the lower left corner of the first sheet so that point A meets with the top edge, while creasing to point B.

2

Fold right side in to meet new edge AB.

3

Fold again as shown. Also fold left edge in as shown.

4

Larger view. Your half wing should look like this.

5

Fold another half wing in the *opposite* direction to your first wing. Now slide the two together. End X slots inside flap Y. Secure the two halves together with tape.

6

Measure ¾" from top point, then fold point down four times.

7

It should look like this. Fold in half behind.

8

Your completed Big Wing. It does not need a fuselage and cuts through the air more efficiently.

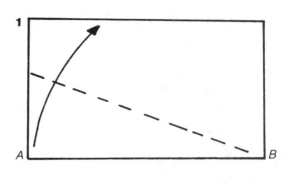

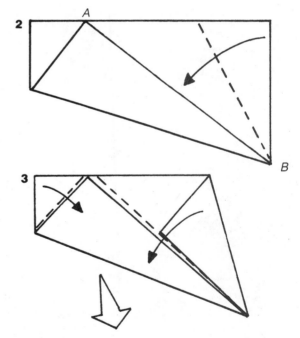

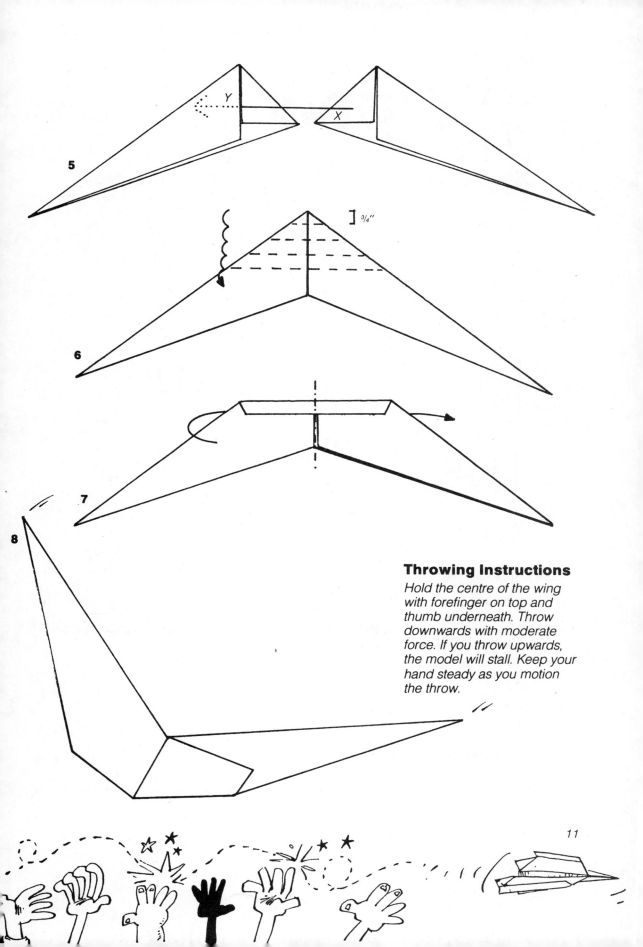

5

X

Y

3/4"

6

7

8

Throwing Instructions

Hold the centre of the wing with forefinger on top and thumb underneath. Throw downwards with moderate force. If you throw upwards, the model will stall. Keep your hand steady as you motion the throw.

Big Zipper

Heads will turn! This is an extremely simple glider that will zip in and out of tight situations, indoors or outdoors. It's versatile too: the tail section can be modified to suit particular stunts.

1

Begin with a sheet of 11"x17" paper facing you as shown, crease folded in half lengthwise. Measure 1⅛" down from the top end then fold the end over and over six times.

2

It should look like this. Fold in half as shown.

3

Larger view, facing you horizontally. The folded end is to the left. Measure 5" in from top right corner. Measure 1" up from bottom right corner. Cut along dotted lines to where they meet at right angles.

4

Measure 1" from top, then mountain fold front fin and valley fold back fin. Measure 1" up from bottom to make fuselage. Fold wings down. Note tail section. This is dealt with in step 5.

5

Inverse fold the tail to make tail wing at desired position **5a** or **5b**.

6

The finished Big Zipper.

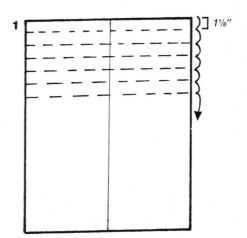

1⅛"

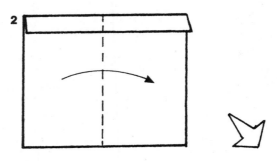

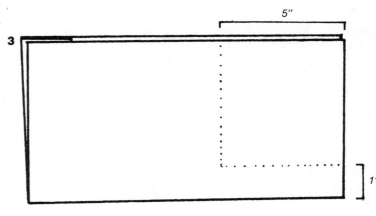

5"

1"

12

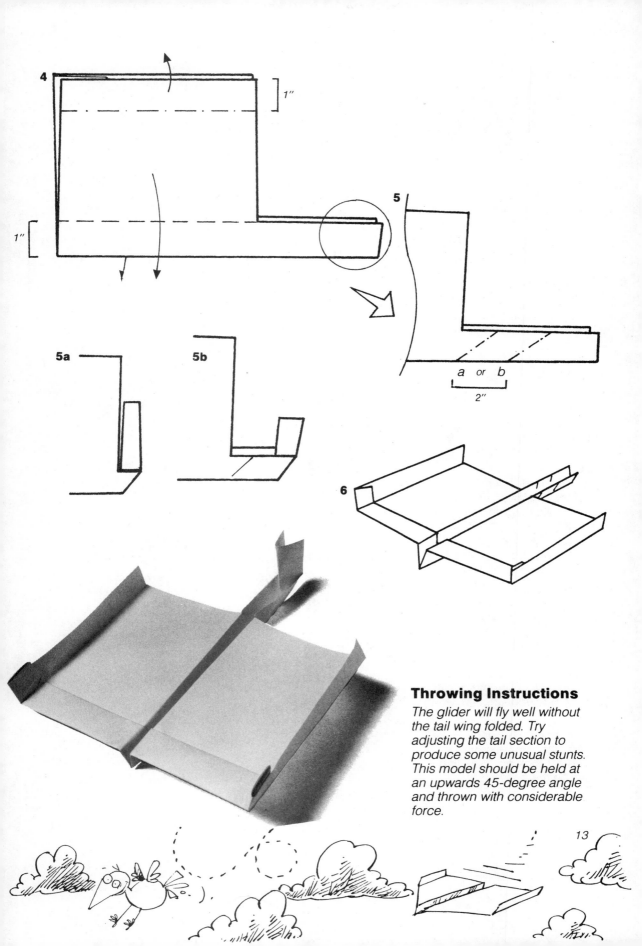

4

1"

1"

5

a or b

2"

5a

5b

6

Throwing Instructions

The glider will fly well without the tail wing folded. Try adjusting the tail section to produce some unusual stunts. This model should be held at an upwards 45-degree angle and thrown with considerable force.

Flying Steeple

Praise the Lord! All churches point to heaven, but this model might just get you there (with a little help from above). It's relatively simple and glides well.

1
Begin with a saintly white sheet of 11"x17", crease folded lengthwise in half. Fold the sides in to meet the centre crease.

2
Fold the top corners in as shown.

3
AB is the same length as AC. Make a diagonal fold so that point B meets point C.

4
Unfold and repeat the procedure by making an opposite diagonal fold so that point A meets point D. Then unfold the model so that it looks like step 5.

5
Your two diagonal folds have made creases which meet at the centre (X). Now fold the lower flaps out along EX and FX. Then make a mountain fold along GXH and bring in points G and H to create a classic 'water bomb' fold (see Folding Techniques page 3).

6
The model should look like this somewhat unpriestly shape. Tuck back the flap inside the nose section.

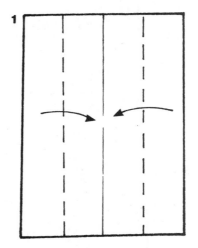

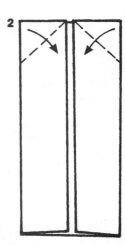

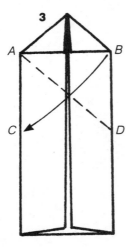

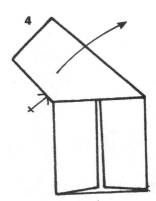

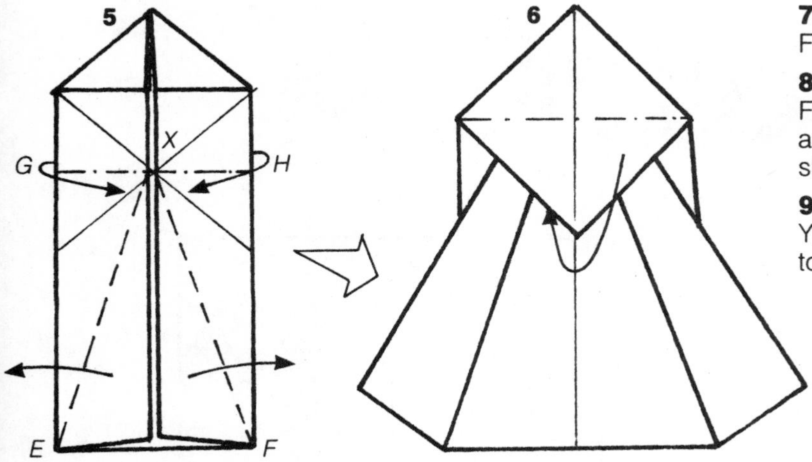

5

6

7
Fold in half behind.

8
Fold wings and fins down in approximate positions as shown.

9
Your Flying Steeple is ready to climb to the heavens.

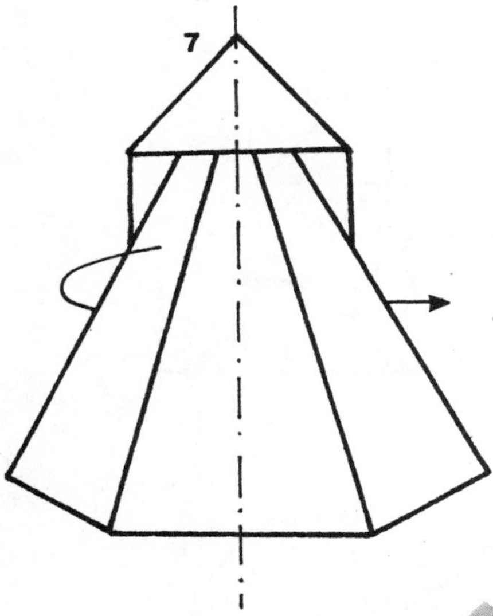

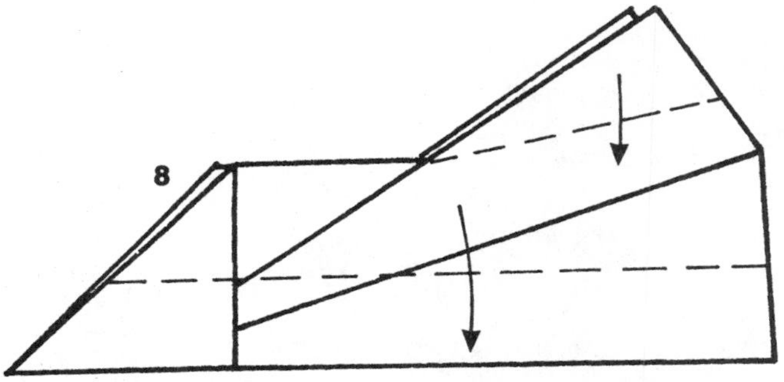

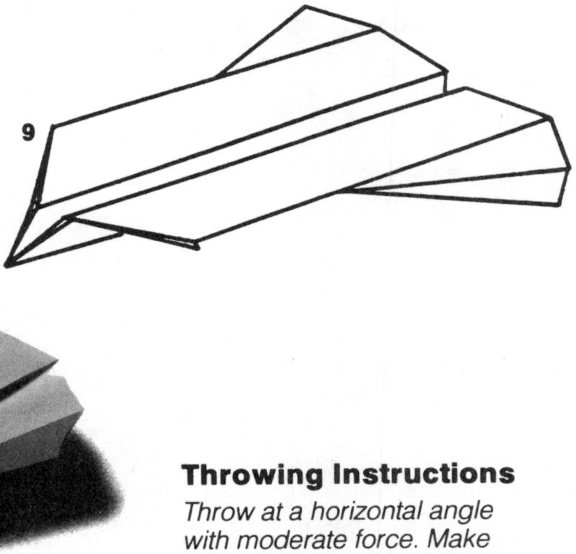

G ⟲ — X — ⟳ H

E F

7

8

9

Throwing Instructions

Throw at a horizontal angle with moderate force. Make sure the wings are level and not drooping down, otherwise your model will roll like a drunk!

15

Easy Glider

This one is so simple, even my cat made one! When he completed the model I awarded him with a sardine. He turned up his nose at me, saying he'd rather have the money. There's just no satisfying anyone these days...

1
Begin with a sheet of 11"x17" facing you horizontally, creased in half widthwise. Fold in the corners.

2
Fold top point down to meet flap edges.

3
A little trickier this (my cat got its claw stuck here): hold A firmly down with your left hand. Place your finger inside, lifting edge BC up and to the left.

3a
Almost there. Flatten the fold. Repeat the procedure for the other side, ensuring exact symmetry.

4
Fold point up to make nose.

5
Fold tip of nose behind edge, locking the fold.

6
Fold in half behind.

7
Fold wings down in approximate position shown.

8
Your Easy Glider doesn't come much easier.

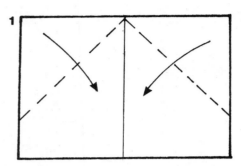

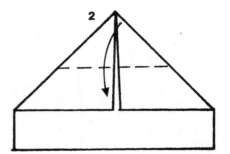

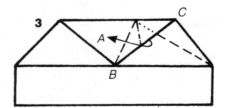

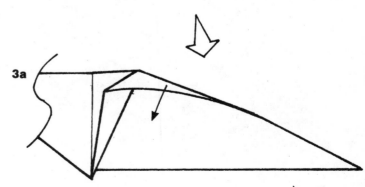

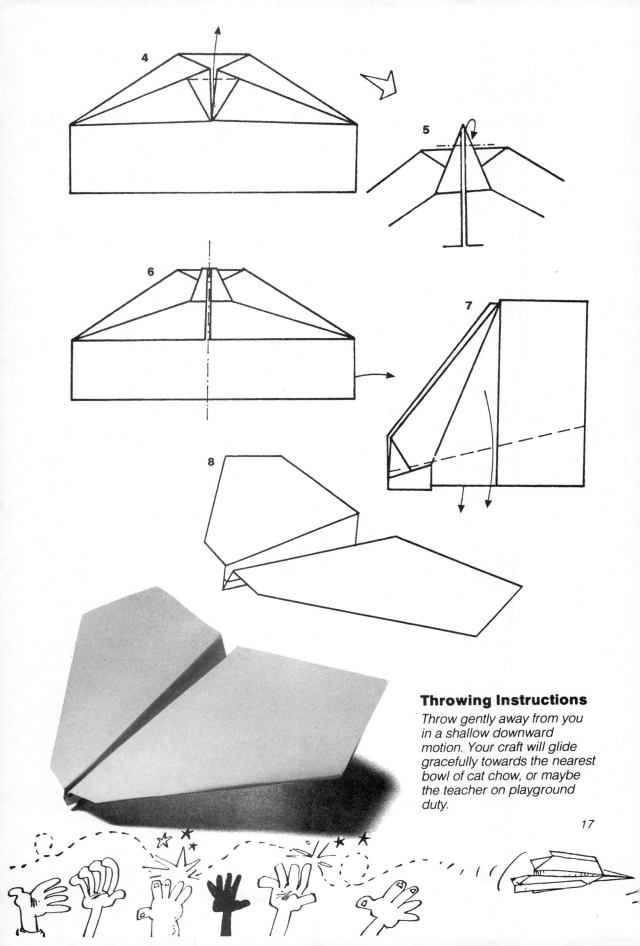

4

5

6

7

8

Throwing Instructions

Throw gently away from you in a shallow downward motion. Your craft will glide gracefully towards the nearest bowl of cat chow, or maybe the teacher on playground duty.

17

Wunda Wing

Throw this and some will wonder where it's gone! This model uses two 11"x17" sheets folded together. You will not need sticky tape.

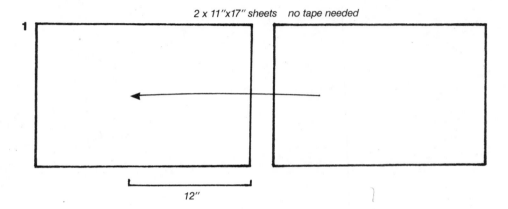

2 x 11"x17" sheets   no tape needed

1

12"

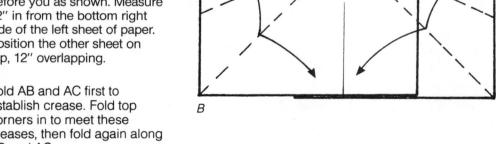

2

A

B

C

1
Place two 11"x17" sheets before you as shown. Measure 12" in from the bottom right side of the left sheet of paper. Position the other sheet on top, 12" overlapping.

2
Fold AB and AC first to establish crease. Fold top corners in to meet these creases, then fold again along AB and AC.

3
Measure 1" from the top point then fold end over and over five times.

4
Fold the model in half behind.

3

] 1"

4

5

crease fold slightly

X ————— X

] 1"

6

5
Crease fold back the wings
along XX but make this
crease a slight one, not well
creased. Measure 1″ up from
the base fuselage and fold the
wings down.

6
Your completed Wunda Wing.

Throwing Instructions

*The folds actually keep the
two 11″x17″ sheets in place.
Hold your arm up high, letting
go of your model with a slight
forward motion. It should glide
well, with surprising stability,
more stable than my ex-
girlfriend!*

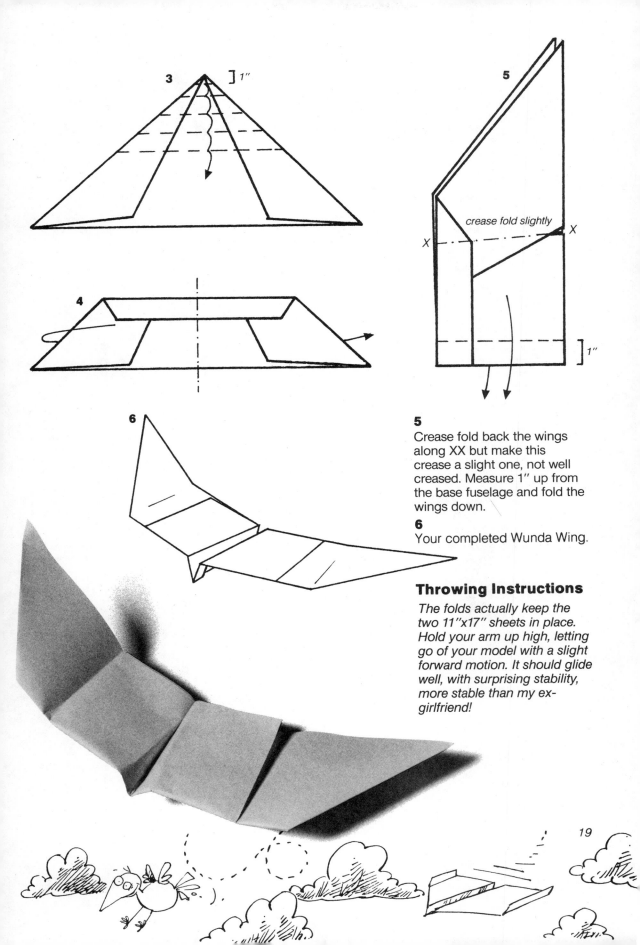

Traditional Glider

This is traditional in the sense that the past ten years have seen remarkable changes in aerogami models and designs. This model is a variation of my previous designs, with more stability and distance achieved — simply by sealing the fuselage!

1

Begin with a sheet of 11"x17" paper, already creased in half lengthwise. Fold the top corners in as shown.

2

Fold top point down to meet bottom edge.

3

Fold point up as shown.

4

Larger view. Bring edge AB to rest alongside BC. Hold the edge down, then place your finger under the entire flap, pushing out the left corner.

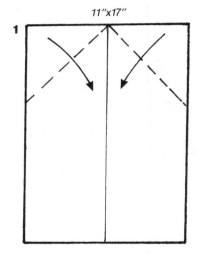

11"x17"

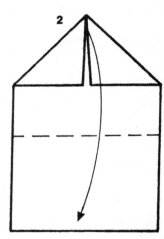

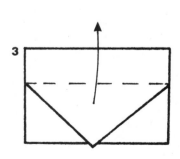

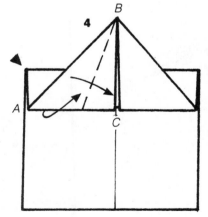

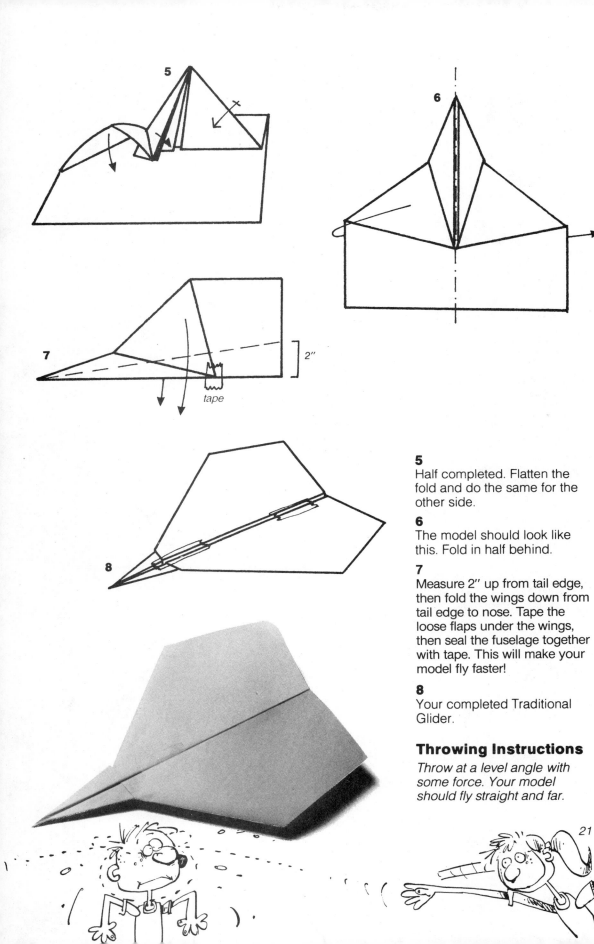

5
Half completed. Flatten the fold and do the same for the other side.

6
The model should look like this. Fold in half behind.

7
Measure 2″ up from tail edge, then fold the wings down from tail edge to nose. Tape the loose flaps under the wings, then seal the fuselage together with tape. This will make your model fly faster!

8
Your completed Traditional Glider.

Throwing Instructions

Throw at a level angle with some force. Your model should fly straight and far.

tape

2″

Dunny Thruster

A flying loo? Not quite! This model combines two empty toilet rolls plus sheets of 11"x17" and 5½"x8½" paper. It will certainly fly further than any bad smell!

1

Join the two rolls lengthwise with tape. Secure firmly. Using scissors, cut horizontal slits in both ends, and parallel slits on the other side, noting measurements.

2

Put the dunny rolls aside for now. Grab a sheet of 11"x17" and fold it into thirds lengthwise.

3

Carefully curl the length of paper to make a circle and tape it closed. This will form the tail wing.

4

Your tail wing section completed.

5

Now take a sheet of 5½"x8½". This will be your nose section. Fold the left corner in as shown.

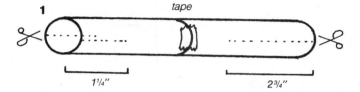

1

tape

1¼"   2¾"

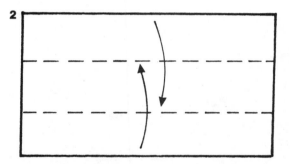

2

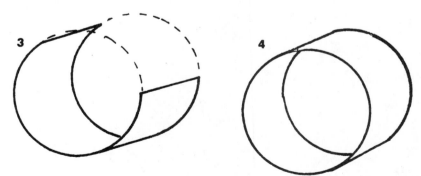

3   4

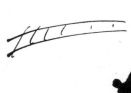

5 5½"x8½"

6

7

8

9

10

6
Fold right corner in as shown.

7
Fold top point down in thirds as shown.

8
Fold sides in. These will be the fins for stability.

9
Remember the empty rolls? If they haven't been flushed already, slot the nose section into the front of the rolls where the insert cut is 1¼". It should fit nicely. Then slot the rear tail circle in the other end as shown.

10
Tape it all together and you are now ready to add a whole new dimension to *Thunderbirds*.

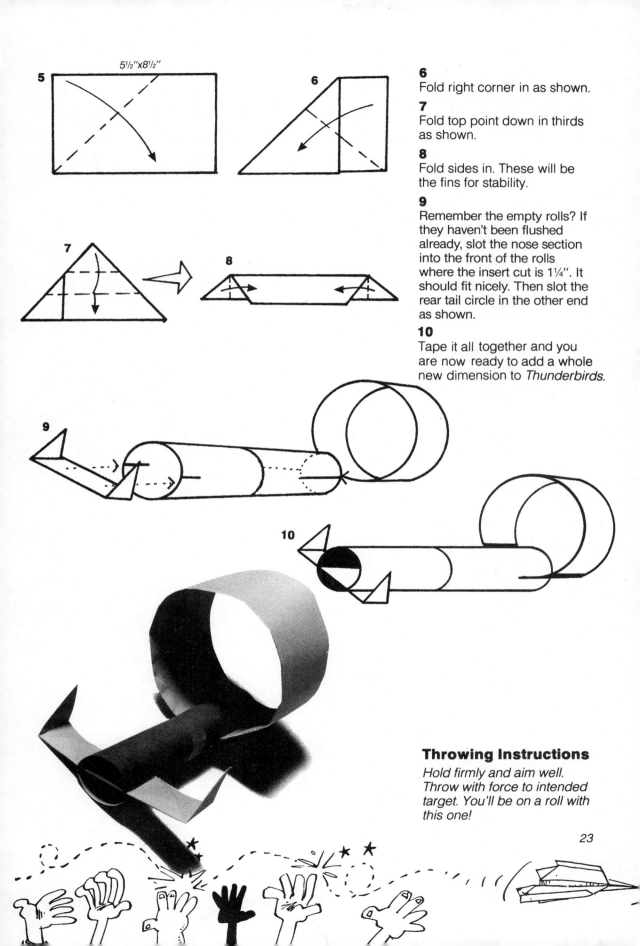

Throwing Instructions

Hold firmly and aim well. Throw with force to intended target. You'll be on a roll with this one!

23

Power Glider

This is the breakfast cereal you throw up! It's made from the cardboard of any large pack of corn flakes, Wheaties, Rice Krispies, etc, etc. The cardboard is solid and, when thrown, travels far. Folding takes a little more effort because the card has to be well creased, but it's worth it.

1
Grab a cereal box — the large pack is preferable — and cut down the glue line to open the box out as shown. Position it flat on the table, glue line to your right. Cut this flap off completely to make the box sides symmetrical. Crease fold in half lengthwise.

2
Fold right flap over along score line.

3
Make a diagonal fold, then open out the top side, pushing in corner A (similar fold to the water bomb base — check your practice model if you haven't thrown it out).

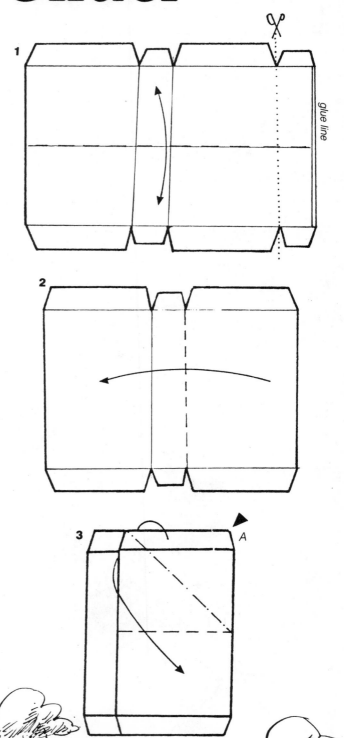

4
Lift new flap up and repeat step 3 for lower half.

5
Measure 3″ from nose, then fold behind. Now fold model in half behind as shown.

6
Larger view. Measure 3″ down and fold landing legs B. Measure 1¼″ down and fold back the tail fins. Measure 1¼″ to 1½″ from base and fold down the wings.

7
Seal the fuselage together with lots of tape.

8
Your Power Glider is ready to power up!

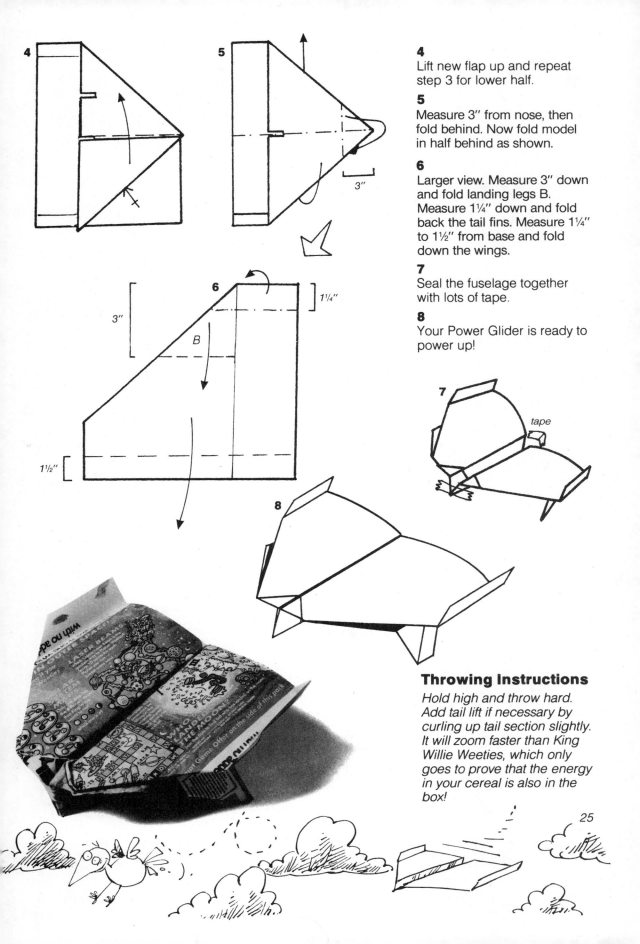

3″

3″

1¼″

B

1½″

tape

Throwing Instructions

Hold high and throw hard. Add tail lift if necessary by curling up tail section slightly. It will zoom faster than King Willie Weeties, which only goes to prove that the energy in your cereal is also in the box!

25

Middleweight Flyer

I'm not talking boxing, but this glider certainly packs a punch when thrown! The weight is concentrated towards the centre of the fuselage making a well balanced glider (more balanced than the author is, anyway).

1
Begin with 11"x17" paper crease folded in half lengthwise. Fold corners in as shown.

2
Fold again as for a classic paper dart.

3
Fold in half behind.

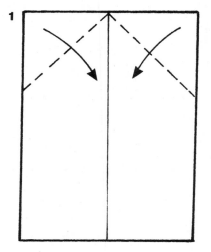

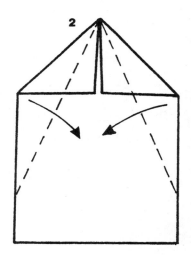

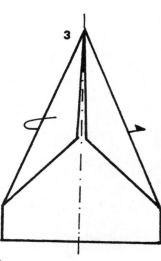

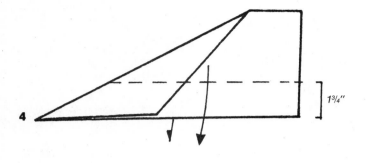

4

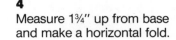

4
Measure 1¾″ up from base and make a horizontal fold.

5
Fold wings up as shown. 'A' is where the crease meets the base of the model.

6
The model is currently folded in half. Unfold and lie flat as shown in step 7.

7
Fold top end down in approximate position shown.

1¾″

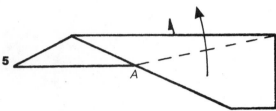

5

A

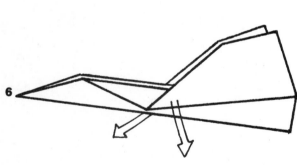

6

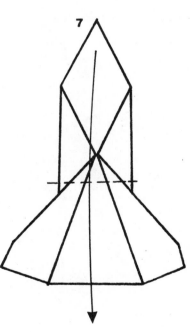

7

8

Fold back up in approximate position shown.

9

It should look like this. Turn the model over.

10

Fold top end down as shown.

11

Fold up again in position shown.

12

Now fold the model in half.

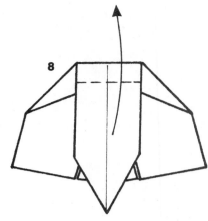

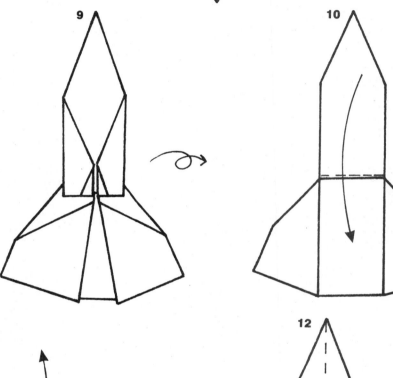

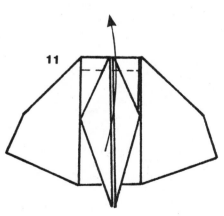

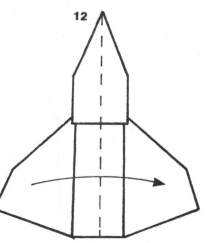

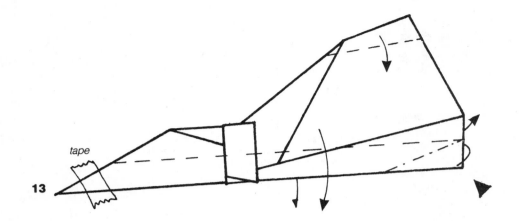

13

Inverse fold the tail section, folding down drop fins and wings. Seal the fuselage together with tape.

14

Your model is ready to fly.

Throwing Instructions

Hold the thick section of the fuselage and throw horizontally with moderate force — it'll knock out the competition!

Manta Ray

Sometimes called 'devilfish', these creatures swim gracefully through warm ocean currents, minding their own business. My Manta Ray happens to fly like an angel, with a wingspan of approximately 28" that will grace any backyard! It uses a strip of card approximately ½" thick for rigidity.

1

You will need three sheets of 11"x17" paper. Position them as shown, so that right and left corners of the two opposing sheets touch the top right and left corners of the centre sheet. Fold the top edge down to where the bottom right and left corners meet.

2

Fold leading edge again to meet the same corner.

3

Fold edge again to meet corner.

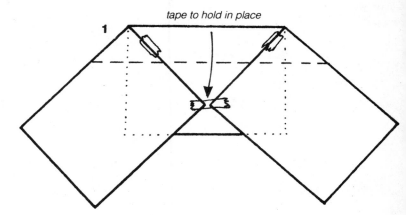

tape to hold in place

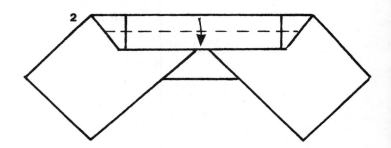

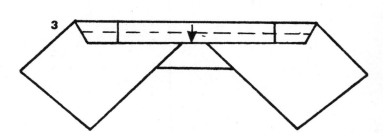

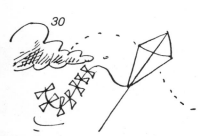

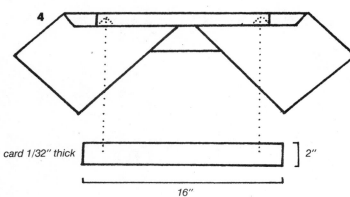

card 1/32" thick

2"

16"

4

Cut out a strip of approximately 1/32" thick card (or
twice the thickness of a manila
folder card), 2"x16". You can
buy the card from any news-
agent or art shop, but a scrap
piece of card from around the
house would be suitable.
Having cut out the card, slot it
under the top folded flap, but
do not tape it together yet.

5

Fold the entire model in half
behind.

6

Larger view. Measure 2" at
front, 3½" at tail, folding the
wings down accordingly.

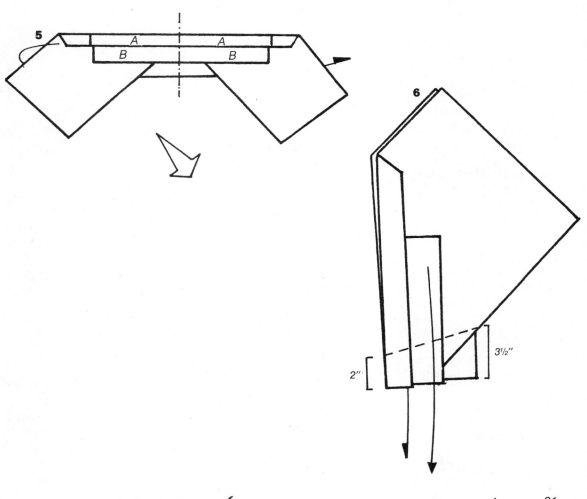

A A
B B

3½"

2"

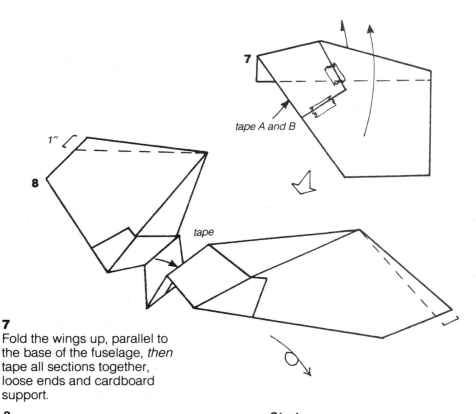

tape A and B

tape

1"

7
Fold the wings up, parallel to the base of the fuselage, *then* tape all sections together, loose ends and cardboard support.

8
Measure 1" back from the wing corners, folding up for lift if necessary. Seal the fuselage together with tape. Secure tightly! The wings will automatically curl as you reinforce the model with tape, giving a natural airfoil.

9
Strut This is an important support for your Manta Ray and will ensure the model does not dive during flight. Grab a strip of paper ¾"x8¼". Fold the corners back, noting measurements, and make a centre crease in the strut.

10
Place your model upside down on a flat surface. Add tape to your strut, attaching it to the underside of your model. Note step 10a for distances.

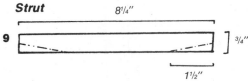

Strut   8¼"

9   ¾"

                    1½"

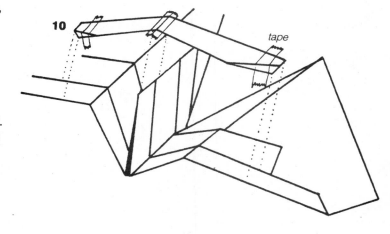

tape